On Brett Favre's helmet
        beer falls, and the cup crumples.
        Sideline in autumn.

TUESDAY MORNING QUARTERBACK

On a withered branch
        a crow has now alighted.
        Nightfall in autumn.

—Matsuo Basho, first haiku master, 1679

On Brett Favre's helmet
        beer falls, and the cup crumples.
        Sideline in autumn.

—Tuesday Morning Quarterback, 2001

TUESDAY
MORNING
QUARTERBACK

**Haiku and Other Whimsical Observations
to Help You Understand the Modern Game**

GREGG EASTERBROOK

UNIVERSE

To my brother, Neil Easterbrook,
who, like me, devotes an unseemly proportion of
his precious time to watching football

First published in the United States of America in 2001
by UNIVERSE PUBLISHING
A Division of Rizzoli International Publications, Inc.
300 Park Avenue South
New York, NY 10010

01 02 03 04 / 10 9 8 7 6 5 4 3 2 1

Printed in Singapore

Design by Dmitry Krasny / Deka Design New York

All photographs in book courtesy of H. Armstrong Roberts, with
exception of image on page 26, courtesy of Image Bank

INTRODUCTION

Ah, for the bygone glory days of football—when lawyers did not stand with players on the sidelines, when 300 pounds was considered big, when fans had beer and hot dogs at their seats instead of cell phones and chicken Caesar wraps, when only the cheerleaders wore earrings.

Ah, for that forgotten, golden age. You know, about five years ago.

Football grows wilder with each passing season. More hype, bigger contracts, more jewelry, sillier controversies, more strutting, less teamwork, louder announcers, higher prices, defensive tackles so huge they should have Zip codes instead of numbers on their jerseys. Ever-larger, ever-faster gentlemen smashing into each other, falling down and getting up to repeat the process. Yet we watch and attend in record numbers each year. So which is worse: football, for steadily getting more outlandish, or us, for staying hooked?

I certainly know I'm hooked. I love everything about football, even the sound effects. I'm so hooked I would watch the Arizona Cardinals play the San Diego Chargers. (Note to those just returning from Mars: these teams went a combined 4–28 during the 2000 season.) Of course, the first step to recovery is admitting you have a problem.

Perhaps the reason football has such appeal is that its preposterousness holds a perfect mirror to early 21st century American society. America, after all, is today a country plagued by hype, exaggeration, excess, showboating, indulgence, litigation, dumbing-down, vainglory, superficiality, sex obsession and spurious media-generated instant scandal. And we're the strongest nation in the world! Perhaps we are strong because we lead the world in hype, exaggeration, excess, showboating, etcetera. If you can succeed despite all these things, then you must have what it takes! And nowhere in today's society are such qualities better exemplified than the cult of football. Exactly because it is so brazenly preposterous, football fascinates us.

Here is an example of the wonderful absurdity of football. During the 2000 season, San Francisco played at Dallas. Niners player Terrell Owens scored a touchdown, then sprinted halfway across the field to dance and preen in the white star at the center of Texas Stadium. Seeing this embarrassing display, Cowboys player George Teague likewise sprinted halfway across the field, then laid Owens out with one of the hardest hits of all time. The hit came a full minute after the whistle had sounded, which does fall somewhat short of ideal sportsmanship.

Yet the sentiment of the football world ran entirely in Teague's favor. Sportscasters everywhere praised him, and my column named him Defensive Player of the Year. Why did football fans side with Teague? Because he had defended the integrity of the game. Technical note: in football terms a man dancing is considered embarrassing, whereas two people slamming into each other violently constitutes dignity.

The book that follows is an attempt to capture some of the preposterous flavor of the modern sport, especially the National Football League, and to offer a few pearls of wisdom about it. Possibly, in some limited cases, just oysters of wisdom.

My own fascination with the sport began when I played college football. All that I will say is that it was at the small-college level, and I certainly played small. This book grows out of my experiences during the 2000 season writing a weekly NFL column, Tuesday Morning Quarterback, for the online publication Slate.com. Here was the best thing about writing a football column: it meant I had to watch every game. As my wife would attempt to plan fall afternoon outings to take the children to picturesque state parks or important cultural events, I would say, "But I have a professional obligation to watch the games!" Why didn't I think of this years ago?

Men of America—and, increasingly, women, according to the demographics—I strongly urge you to start a weekly football column, or at least pretend to do so. Email your column to acquaintances or mimeograph copies and scatter them at the local Dunkin Donuts. Then you can say to your exasperated wife/husband/girlfriend/boyfriend/partner-in-a-committed-relationship, "But I have a professional obligation to watch these games!" Trust me, it works.

In addition to oysters of wisdom—possibly, in some limited cases, anchovies of wisdom—this book offers football haiku. They are best read after entering a contemplative state or, alternatively, after consuming nachos and microbrewed half-dark raspberry light pale ale and watching football on TV. No doubt you have been asking yourself, "When will someone publish a book containing really insightful haiku about the NFL?" At last, your wish has come true.

Gregg Easterbrook
Bethesda, Maryland

P.S.: In composing the haiku, I have followed this strict standard: literary merit optional.

AN ODE TO THE MOST IMPORTANT PLAYER IN NFL HISTORY

Each year when the fumbles, hype and folly of the NFL begin anew, all true fans ought to pause to honor the most important player in pro football history. We speak, of course, of Preston Ridlehuber.

Ah, Ridlehuber. Preston may not quite make it to Canton, but someday he will ascend to the halls of Asgard, where great athletes will celebrate his arrival with song and feasting and the recounting of noble deeds. Or deed, in this case.

Preston Ridlehuber was the hero of the greatest single NFL play of all time, at least from the standpoint of the modern fan. The day was November 17, 1968. The nationally televised game pitted the New York Jets against the Oakland Raiders, at a time when Joe Namath was the talk of football. It was also a time, so dimly remembered, when nationally televised NFL football games were rationed to one per week.

The Jets had just kicked a field goal to take a 32–29 lead with fifty seconds left; Oakland was driving. The clock ticked to 7 p.m. E.S.T., the old, highly formalized starting moment for prime time. Without comment, the football scene dissolved, to be replaced by a gauzy image of *ein kleines Mädchen* collecting flowers in the Swiss Alps as someone yodeled.

Yes, it was "The Heidi Game." Millions of viewers were outraged by the substitution of wholesome family entertainment for the crunching, mindless violence they had been enjoying. They called local TV stations to get the final result, and were stunned to learn the Raiders put up two touchdowns in the final forty-nine seconds to win 43–32. The decisive moment? A wild fumble that was kicked, booted, muffed, and scrummed by countless gentlemen until carried to the end zone by the most important player in NFL history, third-string Oakland halfback Preston Ridlehuber.

Ridlehuber's subsequent accomplishments may have lacked distinction—his final career stats show twelve rushes, four receptions, one punt return and one pass completion. But learning of the Raiders' comeback and knowing they had missed the good part drove the nation's viewers into mass frenzy. Station switchboards were inundated. Within hours of "The Heidi Game," both networks then covering the NFL announced that henceforth they would never cut away from a contest. This established national consensus on an essential precedent: *Nothing is more important than football.*

No cutting away, no matter what! It can be Green Bay 48, Cincinnati 3 late in the fourth quarter of a lightning-delayed game, yet we will see every tick, even if at that moment the Pope is reading a homily pronouncing mandatory premarital sex, or if the White House is announcing a nuclear strike against Belgium.

For we live today in the world Preston Ridlehuber made: a world of weekly national double-headers and regional cards; Monday, Sunday, and Thursday night games; Saturday double-headers in December. Every game played everywhere, for those in the elect with DirecTV. As you ease back into the couch on opening day, with your genetically engineered corn chips and boysenberry-honey half-light microbrewed ale-cider blend, utter a word of thanks to the man who made all this possible.

FOOTBALL HAIKU:

> Runner in the clear,
> heading for six. An instant
> of suspended time.

> He drops back and looks.
> Counts in his head, "One, two, three…"
> Then—*gaccccccckkkkkkkkkkkk*! Sees but turf.

Constitution grants
life, liberty and pursuit
of them braggin' rights.

Turnover city.
Who-dat rookies. Yet they charge
for preseason games.

THE HORROR OF PRESEASON GAMES

Though there can never be too much coverage of real football games, the NFL league and the networks continue to waste valuable time on the meaningless preseason. Not even sports nuts should tune in to NFL preseason games, which are unsightly and pointless. In every preseason game, who-dat rookies and soon-to-be-vanished journeymen collide while coaches call bland "vanilla" plays so as not to give away true strategy. Let's put it this way: You don't want to watch Cindy Crawford shaving her legs, you want to watch her modeling the lingerie. This should be the attitude about football preparation, too.

What is the point of warm-ups before paid audiences and on television? Performers should rehearse in private. There is no Lyric Opera preseason, in which the sopranos hit false notes to try to confuse scouts from other operas. There is no American Ballet Theatre preseason, in which dancers leap into the air but refuse to come down so as not to give away true choreography. There is no Stratford-upon-Avon preseason, in which Hamlet and Ophelia are played by recent drama school dropouts who will be released the following day. The NFL preseason should be reduced to two games or eliminated altogether. The sooner the better to allow everyone to dial in real games and wallow in the pleasantly addled stupor that the true NFL season induces.

BOYS PLAYING A BOYS' GAME

One of the primary illusions of pro football—indeed, all professional sports—is that we are watching men play a boys' game.
In truth, we are watching boys play a boys' game.

Pro athletes may be men in the chronological sense, but otherwise
they are prolonged adolescents with elevated testosterone levels
and pockets stuffed with too many C-notes. There's nothing wrong
with living a prolonged adolescence; we should all be so fortunate.
But we ought not to view athletes as grown-ups engaged in any
kind of real-world struggle. Children may look up to football
players because from the standpoint of a child, a 24-year-old who
chases a ball for a living is a man. Adults should not make this
same mistake.

Similarly, we should not look on pro athletes as heroes or praise
them for courage. Though demanding and physically taxing,
what happens on the field of sports is artificial and unrelated to
the kinds of true courage shown by men and women in law
enforcement, the military, health care, teaching—or parenting.
Pro athletes are entertainers. Being an entertainer is a respec-
table profession, but it's not heroic, and swelling courage is not

required to accept a multimillion-dollar paycheck. To enjoy the performances of athletes with perspective, we should drop any illusion that we are seeing anything other than performances. Be a fan of the entertainment, but save your admiration for the real heroism that does not happen on network television.

Sorry about this slip into sincerity. *It won't happen again.*

One tick left, need six.
        The Hail Mary launched, flies...*clang*.
        Must go to church more.

Cross-wind wafting from
the tunnel end. Kick's up—*doink*.
Teeth gnash, garments rent.

Fans, players, coaches
all concur to detest this:
The salary cap.

Arrives in white stretch,
preposterous full-length fur:
The first-round draft choice.

GO, FIGHTING ARTICHOKES!

Rams, Steelers, Vikings—NFL nicknames sure are serious.
Then there are the slightly less somber college appellations.
Among the best:

- The Blue Hose of Presbyterian College. Refers not to melancholy courtesans, but leggings.
- The Blue Hens of Delaware University. How do you cheer up a blue hen? Goose her!
- The Banana Slugs of the University of California-Santa Cruz. Yes, it's real. Fans chant, "Go, Slugs!"
- The Anteaters of the University of California-Irvine. No word on pregame meals.
- The Gorillas of Pittsburgh of Kansas State, "Home of the Nation's Only Gorillas." Pitt State men's teams have long been Gorillas; the women's squads voted in 1989 to adopt the name too, abandoning their former appellation, Gussies. Missing their chance to become the Hussies!
- The Gamecocks of South Carolina, who get a nod because the women's teams bravely call themselves the Lady Gamecocks despite the extremely common ellipsis of that phrase. Their mascot is even named Cocky, and presumably is male. But this being the 21st century, who knows who's under that costume and what she may be wearing?

·The Fighting Artichokes of Scottsdale Community College. Man, you don't want to get into a beef with a fighting artichoke.

·The Ichabods of Washburn University. Ichabod Crane, as you may remember from the story, was a scheming cad who ended up being murdered by a rival disguised as a headless horseman.

·The Geoducks ("gooey-ducks") of Evergreen State. Geoducks—actually clams—are obscure and repulsive to boot.

All colleges are missing their chance to adopt this nickname set: the men's teams would be the Tarzans and the women's teams would be the Janes. You know who the mascot would be, and the science department could conduct genetic engineering experiments on him. A lot of student-athletes would feel pretty good about taking the field with a glowing, forty-foot-high chimpanzee rooting them on.

Then there is the question of whether any team actually has the delicious nickname Fighting Quakers. Several schools, including Earlham, Guilford and the University of Pennsylvania, are commonly known as the Fighting Quakers. Sadly, Quakers is the official name in each case.

Finally, what does Friends University of Wichita call its teams? Sadly, they are the Falcons, not the Fighting Friends.

For the original Cleveland Browns:

They are back — sort of.
They're brown, anyway. The Browns
Release 2.0.

Drip, drip, drip. Drip, drip.
Quick short, quick short, more quick short.
The West Coast offense.

For the real Baltimore team, the Colts:

Johnny Unitas,
wearing a purple cap? Arrggghhhhh!
Should be blue and white.

For the Buffalo Bills' Super Bowl streak:
Four straight tries, four Ls.
              Nobody ever choked worse.
              Permanent bummer.

THE FOOTBALL-POOL MYSTERY

As the season cranks up, workplace football pools get serious. Just one question for those who participate: Do you know anyone who's ever actually *won* the pool?

Some smiling, friendly guy in your office—one of those guys who, well, you're not sure what he docs, but he always seems busy—hands out the sheets and then collects them with your untraceable cash. Jovial co-conspirators work the rest of the building, factory or campus. The weekend comes and goes and you didn't win, but then neither did anyone else around. It's hard to complain—even if you keep a record of your picks, you have no realistic way of knowing whether someone did better.*

Turns out you never actually meet anyone who won the pool anywhere in your business, school, city, county, Standard Metropolitan Statistical Area or for that matter in the Northern Hemisphere. Next Thursday, though, the guy is back, handing out the sheets again, smiling. You bet he's smiling!

*Some football pool sheets list the previous week's winner at the bottom. For the one that circulates in my office, the previous winner's name is, by the strangest coincidence, always smudged and illegible.

Before the noon hour
beer and ribs, consumed standing.
Marvelous tailgate.

Three-and-out again.
Heads hang, fans boo. Can you fire
coach during the game?

Decibels off scale.
Couldn't hear a jet plane land.
Must be third and long.

It's just inches short.
Commence the chant: "Go! Go! Go!"
Damned if you do and....

TOUCH FOOTBALL SCRIPT

Many successful pro teams use "The Script," a Bill Walsh idea: they come into each game with a script of the first fifteen plays to call. Denver, Green Bay and San Francisco have used a Script approach in recent seasons. All had potent offenses and all won a Super Bowl. Given this success, why doesn't every team use a Script approach? Your guess is as good as mine. (Technical note: this means you will be wrong.) As a public service, here is a Script anyone can use in the version of the sport that regular enthusiasts play—namely, touch football:

1. Any crossing pattern
2. Everybody run a quick out
3. Everybody go deep
4. Any crossing pattern
5. Everybody buttonhook
6. You run a pump-and-go; everyone else do something on the other side
7. Reverse pass back to the QB
8. Any crossing pattern
9. Go deep and I'll deliberately underthrow it
10. Hook-and-ladder left
11. Quick snap as soon as we get to the line
12. Any crossing pattern
13. Act like you're mad because you're not going to get the ball, then I'll hit you
14. Direct snap to anyone
15. Quarterback draw on three Mississippi

Repeat as necessary. Stop periodically to drink microbrewed strawberry-blonde unfiltered wheat-based dark pale ale.

"HE'S WIDE OPEN ON A DOUBLE REVERSE AND THEY'RE GIVING 110%!"

"*He's wide open!*" Viewers hear this constantly, though receivers described as *wide open!* are often tackled as they catch the ball. To announcers there seem to be two possible conditions for a receiver: covered or *wide open!* But watch a game in person and you'll see that players are almost never wide open; they either have a slight edge on their pursuer in man-coverage, or are free for an instant in the seam of a zone, with hostile individuals bearing down on them.

Announcers endlessly say *wide open!* both out of hyperventilation and because they aren't taking in the full field. Rather, they are squinting at the little TV-sized tetragon where the ball is—an edited perspective that artificially exaggerates the distance between runner and defender. Even good offenses are lucky if, once a game, a receiver breaks free of coverage altogether— usually, on a blown assignment. But in the announcer's world, every third pass goes to someone *wide open!*

Other infuriating announcer tics:

· "It's a double reverse!" Probably no NFL team in the modern era has run an actual double reverse—a play on which there's a handoff in one direction, a second handoff coming the opposite way, and then a third handoff back to the original direction. NFL defenders are so fast that in the time it takes a double reverse to develop, players from games held the previous week will have closed on the ball carrier. What announcers call a "double reverse" is usually a single reverse, and what announcers call a "reverse" is usually an end-around—a play in which the quarterback hands to an end running parallel to the line, but the ball itself never changes direction. True, defensive players yell "REVERSE!" when they see this action, but only because it is cumbersome to yell "END-AROUND!" Announcers should use correct terminology.

·"He's giving 110 percent." Wouldn't it be nice to have the extra 10 percent from all those gentlemen who give more than is physically possible?

·"He's got athleticism." This phrase appears to mean "he is athletic," or perhaps refers to a disease.

·"Right now somebody needs to step up and make a play." Somebody always needs to make a play.

·"This is a bad time for a turnover." When precisely *is* a good time?

·"They didn't need that penalty." When *do* they need a penalty?

• "He's taking it to another level." This appears to mean "he's playing better," if it means anything. (Note: elevator operators take it to another level.)

• "They have to win this football game." Don't we already know it's a *football* game? Announcers seem to think adding the superfluous adjective *football* makes statements stronger: coaches must be "football coaches," players are not just players but "football players." It's only a matter of time until some announcer refers to "the football ball."

Perhaps most annoying is the "he could have _____" construction, as in, "If no one had tackled him, he could have gone all the way!" Of course if the player hadn't been tackled or hadn't fumbled or hadn't fallen down at the snap, he "could have" done something else. Many players about whom announcers shriek "he could have gone all the way" stood little chance of gaining more than a few extra yards if you view the entire field, not the TV tetragon that makes the ballcarrier appear to be alone.

Clichés in steady
    stream. Hyperventilation.
    The boys in the booth.

Look this way please and
    tell us about your fumble.
    Sideline reporter.

TRAGICALLY MISPLACED NETWORK PRIORITIES

I don't know about you, but I've had my fill of sideline "reaction" shots of coaches. From these all-too-frequent views, we have learned: 1) When something good happens, coaches smile and 2) when something bad happens, they frown. Or, they show no emotion at all, and is that ever interesting! Many coach reaction shots are such zoom-ins the information content is mainly cosmetology.

Scientists estimate that approximately 48 million viewers could do with fewer views of red-faced coaches engaged in pointless yakking duels with the zebras (was there a single call in any game in football annals that a coach didn't holler about?) and increased camera focus on the cheerleaders. The cheerleaders, after all, are *supposed* to be looked at.

NFL cheerleaders spend months intensively preparing to be viewed; it is their raison d'être. Aesthetically, many achieve exceptional results: the cheerleading units of the Dallas Cowboys, Miami Dolphins and Oakland Raiders are particularly distinguished. Yet although television is desperate for visual allure, the NFL networks show 200 disagreeable shots of neck veins bulging on an angry coach for every one view of the highly agreeable cheerleaders. When cheerleaders do get their brief flicker of camera time, usually it is with advertiser logos plastered over their most aesthetically appealing features, during "bridge" shots out of commercials. The courage, devotion and professionalism of football cheerleaders is one of the great untold stories of our time. Why don't the networks reward these dedicated women by letting viewers see the results of their hard-working preparation? (Okay, and let them see the dance routines too.)

ON CHEERLEADERS:

The cheerleaders' skirts
     can never be short enough.
     Please, another gust.

The cheerleaders' tops
can never be low enough.
          Please, lean forward soon.

                    Yes, great dance routines.
          Your professionalism
               we also admire.

FAKE KICK = VICTORY

Science searches for immutable, underlying laws of nature. Searching for the immutable, underlying laws of football, I kept pad and pencil at my side throughout the 2000 NFL season and determined this: there is nearly a one-to-one relationship between executing a successful fake kick and winning a football game.

For example, on one Sunday in October 2000, the Bills, Eagles, Jets, Rams and Saints all executed successful fake kicks and won; no losing team converted a fake. One Sunday in November 2000, the Bears, Bucs and Dolphins all ran successful fake kicks and won; no losing team converted a fake kick. The following week the Colts, Cowboys, Eagles, Rams and Tampa Bay all executed fake kicks and won. In the case of Dallas, the margin of victory turned out to be a fake in which the ball ended in the hands of a scrawny placekicker who ran *up the middle* for a touchdown. To my knowledge, only one NFL team in 2000 ran a successful fake kick and lost. The Packers fell to the Bucs in a game where this law of nature was disturbed because Tampa Bay, too, called a fake kick. NFL coaches, live a little—fake a kick!

REGULAR PASS ≠ VICTORY

Here's another immutable law of football: when you get to the goal line, you *must not* throw regular passes from regular passing sets. Regular pass plays don't work at the goal line because the closer the offense gets to the end zone, the less territory the defense must protect: by the time the ball is on the one yard line, it's nearly impossible for a receiver to get open on a regular pattern. During the 2000 season, teams that ran regular pass plays from in close consistently came to woe. One reason the defending champion Rams sputtered is that they lost consecutive close games to the Redskins and Saints; in the fourth quarter of both contests, the Rams threw interceptions when attempting regular pass plays at the goal line.

The sorts of plays that work at the goal line are power runs, roll-outs and play-fakes from a "jumbo" set—actions in which the team lines up for a power run then throws a quick flip to a tight end or other seeming blocker. If by chance you should become an NFL offensive coordinator, please keep this in mind.

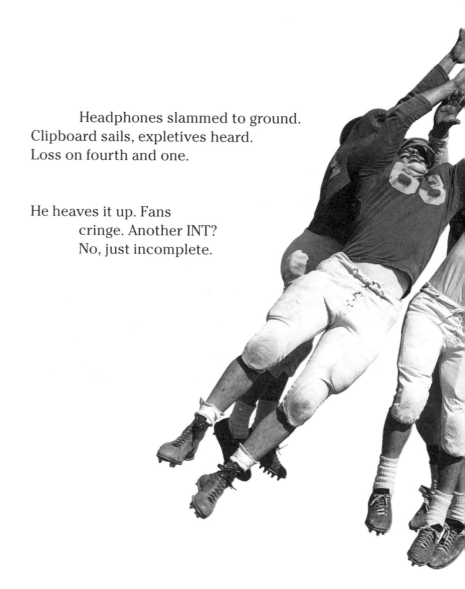

Headphones slammed to ground.
Clipboard sails, expletives heard.
Loss on fourth and one.

He heaves it up. Fans
cringe. Another INT?
No, just incomplete.

All walk back, are glum.
      Football's most tedious play:
      offside on a punt.

A fumble bounces.
Prompt Pavlovian response:
      Must fall on the ball!

Touchdown! The crowd roars!
    Wait, what's that fleck of yellow?
    Oh, no. Not again.

                Me? Excuse me, sir!
            On me? That call was on me?
            On me? I'm speechless!

The rusher breaks free,
                    then suspicious fall. "*Holding.*"
Ref, he must have slipped!

"On further review…"
Stares into box, hems and haws.
Might as well flip coin.

BUCK-BUCK-BUCK-BRAWCKKKKKKK!

Why do NFL coaches order punts when their teams are far behind, or trailing late? College coaches have reason to do this: since team rankings are based partly on scoring margins, it can make sense to punt in order to prevent a close defeat from turning into a blowout. But the only form of ranking in the pros is the W–L ratio—if you're behind late or trailing big, what possible good does a punt accomplish? Why not go for it and at least have a chance on a comeback?

Yet punting when behind is the rule. A few of just many examples from the 2000 NFL season: The sad Chicago Bears, with nothing to lose at a record of 2–7, trailed the Bills by ten points with five minutes left in the game and…punted. The Dallas Cowboys, miserable at 4–6, trailed the Ravens by seventeen in the third quarter, faced a fourth-and-inches at midfield and…punted. In a game they needed to make the playoffs, the Jets trailed Oakland by twenty-one late in the second quarter, faced fourth and two at midfield and…punted. In a game they needed to make the play-offs, the Dolphins, trailing Tampa with three minutes to play, faced fourth and three in Tampa territory and…punted. All of the timorous punting teams went on to lose.

Strange punting behavior can be seen even in the postseason, when there's no tomorrow. In the January 2001 Miami at Oakland playoff game, the Dolphins trailed the Raiders by twenty in the third quarter, faced fourth and short and…punted. Down by twenty you've got to take some chances, and there aren't gonna be many chances better than fourth and short. In the January 2001 NFC championship game, Minnesota trailed the New York Giants by twenty-four points late in the second quarter, faced fourth and inches and…punted. Down by twenty-four you've got to take some chances, and there is no chance better than fourth and inches. Why didn't they try for a last gasp? Better to go down in flames than go down punting.

STOP ME BEFORE I BLITZ AGAIN!

Crowds scream, "Blitz! Blitz!" Announcers and the sports media adulate the blitz. Purists scream, "Don't blitz!" A few blitz vignettes from the 2000 NFL season:

· Detroit faces third and eight against the Giants. Odds favor the defense, as the average NFL pass attempt yields 6.2 yards. All New York needs to do is play straight defense and get a stop. Instead, it's a blitz! The Giants send seven. Lions receiver Johnny Morton is uncovered for the 32-yard touchdown that ices the game.

· Pittsburgh has Tennessee on the ropes, down by a point with 2:11 remaining and facing fourth and eight with only one time-out left. The Steelers force an incompletion and the game's over. Instead, it's a blitz! The blitz leaves a man uncovered; Tennessee quarterback Steve McNair calmly throws for seventeen yards, setting up the winning field goal.

· In the single most disastrous play of the 2000 season, Baltimore at Oakland for the AFC championship, no score, the Raiders have the Ravens backed up on their own four, facing third and 18. All Oakland has to do is play straight defense, get a stop and great field position would await. Instead, it's a blitz! Baltimore tight end Shannon Sharpe takes a short pass 96 yards for a touchdown and the Raiders never recover.

Of course there are instances when blitzes work. But have a pad and pencil handy next time you watch an NFL contest—keep track, and you'll see that blitzing is more likely to turn third-and-long into a first down for the offense than it is to cause a sack or turnover. During the 2000 season, none of the NFL's top three defenses—Tennessee, Baltimore and Buffalo—played a blitz-oriented scheme. (Tennessee's "46" defense often looks like it's blitzing when it is not: linebackers go after the QB, but only a total of four players are rushing.) Meanwhile some of the league's worst defenses, including 21st-ranked Indianapolis, blitzed constantly. Blitzing makes the crowd roar and the booth announcers swoon. But sophisticated coaches know that the *clang* of an incomplete pass is often the sweetest sound to a defense, and usually the best way to get that *clang* is to drop back into coverage.

THE SIESTA SECRET

Sure, it's great to watch football on Sunday afternoons. But let's come clean about the true motive of many viewers: a good nap.

Repetitive down-and-outs, lulling three-yard plunges, the comforting assurance of knowing the announcers will never say anything original—what could be a better prescription for drifting off into dreamland? This is why I recommend watching the NFL in a quiet, cool, softly lit environment, with the phone disconnected. Get comfy in a recliner. Ideally, this should be an old, beat-up recliner with frayed upholstery and exposed stuffing; it took me the better part of a decade to break in my own favorite football recliner. Set out a nice platter of asiago'n'ranch–sprayed genetically engineered corn chips, and pour an up-to-date drink such as a frozen blueberry-almond martini. Sip and munch. Turn the volume low. Slip into a pleasing stupor. If anything really important happens, the crowd noise will wake you.

FOR TODAY'S FAN:

Remote, snacks, beer, dip
all ready. Sound asleep by
the second quarter.

Where's that darn remote?
Found, click. Shoot, dropped it again.
Two games on at once.

THE REAL DIFFERENCE
BETWEEN MEN AND WOMEN

"But it's The Big Game!"
"But it's The Big Sale!"

Variations on this theme are common in my house in the autumn. Looking at the week's lineup of televised football tilts, everything always seems Big to me—*Panthers at Chargers on Fox, wow! Wabash at Pittsburgh of Kansas State on ESPN 9, whew! These look big!* Plaintively I tell my wife, "But it's The Big Game!"

Regrettably she has been perusing the same newspaper and finding similarly cosmic entries—*Twenty percent off our entire selection of mismatched imported pumps, holy smokes! That looks big!* Insistently she informs me, "But it's The Big Sale!"

Since, as we are now told, all human behavior is determined by genetics, I suspect the presence of gender-specific superficiality genes. There must be a DNA sequence on the male (Y) chromosome that makes every game a Big Game, and a parallel sequence somewhere on the X chromosome (double Xs cause a female) that codes every sale as a Big Sale. One shudders to speculate on which of these genes is dominant.

FOR THE PLAYERS, BY POSITION:

Can't use bathroom scale
Press guide lists weight estimate.
The modern DT.

Over the middle
not safe for lean WRs.
All want down-and-outs.

Hit whatever moves.
Make someone pay for each catch.
We are the LBs.

Nameless, they fire out.
Anonymous, they protect.
The offensive line.

Ideally, don't play.
Fans wince when I trot on field.
I am the punter.

    Big and fast but not
As big or as fast. Okay,
You can play tight end.

Shoulder-down lead blocks.
        Carries but once a season.
        I am the fullback.

Plays for the big sack.
Stop toss? Stop draw? What's that mean?
The modern DE.

A physique that seems
genetic'ly engineered.
Today's running back.

My opponent's back
Clear view of his name, number.
The DB's nightmare.

The kicker lines up.
One swing, win or lose. Don't let
that make you nervous.

The biggest bonus.
　　　Interviews and endorscments.
　　　I am the QB.

NEWTON'S THIRD LAW OF NFL MOTION

San Francisco and Dallas met for some of the best, most tense, and most important games of recent decades, including stirring NFC championship matchups. In the 2000 season, the Niners and the Cowboys played a terrific game full of exciting plays—and no one cared, because when it was over, the clubs were a combined 2–6. The two clubs closed out the year a combined 11–21. San Francisco had 122 wins, the most of any NFL team during the 1990s, while Dallas tied Buffalo for second with 113. But by the turn of the millennium, both storied franchises were gasping for air, while Baltimore and Tennessee, teams that didn't even exist a few years ago, were monopolizing headlines.

This demonstrates Newton's Third Law of NFL Motion: For every lesser team that gets hot, there must be an equal and opposite great team that goes in the tank.

Man deep uncovered,
seen by all except QB.
How he dreads the film.

Blood on pillowcase.
Ev'ry cell in body hurts.
Morning after game.

INSERT HEAD. OBEY COACH.

Viewers who squint at the TV tube may notice that printed on the back of every NFL helmet is a block of disclaimer text warning players about the chance of injury. Logically, warnings are only relevant to those unaware of risks; if there's an NFL player so dense he does not know football is dangerous, some lawyer-written gibberish on the helmet is unlikely to do him much good. But as a public service, here is what actually appears in that unreadable block of helmet text:

Instructions

Insert head. Obey coach. Give 110 percent. (If not presently giving 110 percent, ask trainer to tighten the screws in your frontal lobes.) Continue every play until such time as you hear the whistle sound, or notice that everyone has left the stadium. When game completed, remove helmet. Repeat sequence until you are waived for a younger, less expensive player.

Warnings

Concussion, torn body parts and intense pain are normal during use of this product. You must sign the release of liability; please do not read the release before signing. Manufacturer not responsible for points scored, bonuses offered or crowd response. Bird claws, lightning bolts or similar mythical imagery on helmet do not confer these properties on wearer. Never use your helmet in a deliberate attempt to injure other players: all attempts to injure other players should appear to be inadvertent. If ringing in ears persists more than five years after your final game, consult a health-care professional. And for goodness's sake be careful—the coffee at your pregame breakfast may be very hot!

EARLY RETIREMENT FOR NUMBERS

After Dan Marino left football, the Dolphins retired his number, making that the second jersey that club has set aside perpetually. As with Miami, most franchises rarely retire a number. For instance the Steelers, despite their 1970s dynasty team, have but one prohibited integer, that of Ernie Stautner. Three clubs—Buffalo, Dallas and Oakland—have never witnessed this ceremony, because they do not retire numbers.

Then there are the Chicago Bears. Numbers 3, 5, 7, 28, 34, 40, 41, 42, 51, 56, 61, 66 and 77 cannot be worn by current Bears because they have been retired in recognition of gentlemen past. And Mike Singletary's number isn't even on that list! This leads to a perpetual number crunch when Chicago is handing out jerseys. Fortunately, in order to avoid making the situation worse, the Bears have a strict team policy of not developing any more great players.

FOR STADIUMS AND TEAMS BYGONE:

For the original Three Rivers:

One team, one decade,
one field, four rings. This will not
happen again soon.

For RFK:

You could feel it shake.
Woe to the opponent who
riled up RFK.

For the original Mile High:

> Thin air, mountain views.
> Visitors, gasping for breath,
> doomed in fourth quarter.

For the soon-to-be-demolished, original Soldier Field:

> Snow and freezing wind
> off lake. Then, weather gets bad.
> Away team shivers.

For Los Angeles:

> Odious agents,
> vacuous bimbos. Yet oh,
> where the NFL?

WHY COACHES SHOULD BE COLD

Attend or watch a cold-weather game, and you can guess in an instant who will win merely by checking attire on the sidelines. Are the coaches dressed like manly men in sweaters or varsity jackets, or are they huddled in ridiculous K2 survival gear?

In the 2000 season, Indianapolis (a dome-based team for whom "cold" is a setting on the air conditioning) went to Green Bay and tried to perform in swirling snow. On the sidelines, Colts coaches wore heavy, McMurdo-base-style parkas with ski caps pulled over the ears; Packers coaches wore varsity jackets and baseball hats. Green Bay won.

Tampa Bay, a Florida team now 0–19 lifetime when the kickoff temperature is below 40°F, went into Chicago at 37°F and honked to the cellar-dwelling Bears. Tampa sideline staff wore not only heavy parkas but balaclavas; they looked like they were preparing to join the Amundsen-Scott expedition. The Arizona (caution: may contain football-like substance) Cardinals left their land of sun and halter-tops and went to Philadelphia, where kickoff temperature was in the 40s and Cardinals coaches wore heavy parkas. Several looked like they were preparing to go EVA to fix the antenna on the Jupiter ship in *2001: A Space Odyssey*. The roasty-toasty Cardinals got clobbered. God help them if the thermometer should dip below 40! Later, Tampa Bay traveled to Green Bay in snow, and again its coaches severely overdressed. The Bucs had a field goal attempt to win on the final play. Tampa kicker Martin Gramatica trotted out in a full-head eye-slit ski mask that made him look like a Jawa from *Star Wars.* He missed—it was a wonder he could even see the ball—and the Packers won in OT.

Ah, for the days of manly man Minnesota coach Bud Grant. Back before the Vikes took their game indoors, Grant allowed the visiting team to have sideline heater units but banned them for his own players, believing it was an advantage to shrug at the cold while others fretted about staying warm. How right he was. Thus two laws of football: Cold Coaches = Victory while Ridiculous K2 Survival Gear ≠ Victory.

Contrapositive proves the rule: when the Dolphins went to Buffalo in the 1999 season, the Miami coaching staff overdressed in ridiculous K2 survival gear while the Buffalo sideline wore sweaters. Final, Bills by 20. Remembering this lesson, in their 2000 appearance at Buffalo, Dolphins coaches wore sweaters, though it was below freezing. Dolphins QB Jay Fiedler came out for warm-ups in shorts. Final, Miami by 27.

Eighty-two thousand.
Faces painted, voices hoarse.
Must be December.

Once playoffs begin
        just one ends year still alive.
        How Darwinian.

THE PERFECT LIBATION

One of the sweetest traditions in sports lore involves the 1972 Dolphins, who finished 17–0, the sole perfect season in NFL annals. Each year, at the moment when the last remaining unbeaten pro football team honks a game, each surviving member of the 1972 Dolphins uncorks a bottle of champagne that he set aside to cool on the current season's opening day. And it's genuine Champagne champagne, not the sparkling Chilean mango chutney–flavored white zinfandel/Gewürztraminer/schnapps blend passing for bubbly thesc days. Gentlemen of 1972, enjoy your annual draught. You earned it. And you are likely to savor these bubbles each autumn until the day the football gods summon you to Asgard for song and feasting.